Robert Garnham is...

Nice

Robert Garnham

Burning Eye

This edition published by Burning Eye Books 2015

www.burningeye.co.uk
@burningeyebooks

Burning Eye Books
15 West Hill, Portishead, BS20 6LG

ISBN 978-1-909136-64-9

Nice

CONTENTS

'Some people have bravery and balls, and they go out into the world and challenge life. They take hold of disappointment and confusion and they turn it all around. And some don't. Did you know that sausages were actually named after sausage dogs? I've lost my train of thought now.'
Professor Zazzo Thiim, 1998

INTRODUCTION: SOME USEFUL TIPS FOR PERFORMING PERFORMANCE POETRY AT PERFORMANCE POETRY PERFORMANCE NIGHTS

1. Sit at the back. Don't sit at the front. If you sit at the front, when it's your turn to perform you'll be performing to an empty chair.

2. Also, if you sit at the back, the audience will clap for longer while you're walking to the microphone.

3. If you are a prop poet and you bring a cow to the stage, don't point out that you've brought a cow to the stage, because people can see that you've brought a cow to the stage.

4. Don't milk it.

5. If you bring books to sell, beg the host for a slot in the first half. That way you can sell books during the interval and still have time to run off and get the train. Make sure you can change a twenty.

6. If someone says they like your stuff, they usually mean it. Sometimes they say it so that you'll automatically reply that you like their stuff, but not always. Sometimes they'll say it because you were awful and they feel sorry for you, but not always. But most of the time they mean it.

7. I mean, I think they do.

8. I'm pretty sure of it but you've got me thinking, now.

9. If it's an open mic, spell your name legibly on the sign-in sheet. I usually end up being announced as Rupert Graham.

10. If you're performing haiku, for God's sake, we all know what haiku are, so you don't have to explain what a haiku is. Syllables and stuff. Explaining what a haiku is usually takes longer than performing the haiku. Sodding haiku.

11. Don't get rat-arsed.

12. If you're using props, check for light fixtures and obstructions.

13. I mean, is it me, or do haiku always seem like they should be longer?

14. If you want to have a laugh while performing, make eye contact only with one audience member, then glare at them, give them the old stare, really freak them out.

15. It's not a competition.

16. Well, except for slams. I forgot about slams.

17. Don't give away all your poem in the introduction.

18. If you bow to the audience at the end of your set, don't bang your forehead on the microphone. It bloody hurts.

19. The long walk back to your seat is still part of the performance. Maintain your aura. Try not to trip over handbags. And listen out, because the compere might make some wise-arse remark about you.

20. Always leave them wanting more. Try to do less than the time allocated. The host will love you for it.

POEM

A pen fell down
The lining of my coat.
It's in there somewhere,
Like a deep sea diver
Exploring the unknown.
It bangs my leg as I walk,
Rhythmically.

Or it goes round the back.

Oh, penny penny pen pen.
The hole down which you fell
Was incredibly small.
Yet down you went
As if disappearing into the mysterious
Limbo of my inner lining
Like a thought nagging
At my conscience,
A half-concealed memory
Long repressed.

An inspiring biro survivor,
That you might never see
The light again.
How willingly do you hide,
Lingering, always there?
It's a good job
I've got a spare.

I asked my friend Anne
And she said, 'We're all
Archaeologists of the present moment,'
And I said, 'That's not helping.'

A pen fell down
The lining of my coat
And now I refer to it as
The Coat With The Pen In The Lining,

So it almost seems a shame now
To try and get it back.

I prayed the other night
And in the morning
Someone had nicked my coat.
They're in for a surprise.

POEM

A pig and a donkey did it once
And now we've got a ponkey.
It stands in the reception area
Next to the receptionist.
It's ever so helpful.

A visiting professor of zoology
Was most bemused by its neurological
Characteristics.
The tenacity of a donkey.
The amiability of a pig.
'The best of both worlds, Mr Morgan,
The best of both worlds.'

And I said,
'Who's Mr Morgan?'
And the ponkey said,
'Squeal-aw.'

One night the receptionist said,
'I can't work properly or efficiently with the ponkey
Watching my every move,'
And I said, 'It's got the amiability of a pig,
That's what the professor said,'
And she replied, 'I wouldn't go trusting
Everything that quack said.
After all, he thought your name was
Mr Morgan.'
Fair point.

A plaice and a flounder did it once
And now we've got a plounder.
It then had offspring of its own
Which are quarter-plounders.
They taste just like flounders.

POEM

I watched the film *Titanic*.
The boat sank.
I watched the film *Titanic*.
The boat sank.
I watched the film *Titanic* again.
And the boat sank again.
I watched the film *Titanic*.
It was three bloody hours long.
It only took the *Titanic* two hours to sink.
So that's one hour of faffing around.

At the start of the film
A man kept saying,
'The *Titanic* is unsinkable.
The *Titanic* is unsinkable.
The *Titanic* is unsinkable.
Unless water cascades over the separating watertight
Bulkheads.'
And then one hour into the film
Water cascaded over the separating watertight bulkheads.
It sank.

'Iceberg. Right ahead.'
That's what the iceberg spotter said.
The moment he spotted an iceberg.
Which was kind of his job.
At least someone was on the ball that night.

Like a gin and tonic,
The *Titanic* went down well
With ice.
Although it was probably a
Quite horrific event.

POEM

The moon isn't really called 'the moon'.
It's actually called Simon.
It's a secret that the astronomers
Don't want us to know
Because they think it's a bit embarrassing
That the moon is really called Simon.
It sounds more like a moustachioed gas boiler
Inspector from Kettering
Than an interplanetary body.

Moon. Simon. Simon. Moon.

1950s.
NASA.
1950s.
NASA.
Let's all ride a rocket ship
To the Simon.
Let's all ride a rocket ship
To the Simon.
Count down, six, five,
Four, three,
Two, one.
Look out, Groovy Simon,
Here we come!

A hop, a skip and a jump
On the surface of Simon.
Poking poking poking around
On the surface of Simon.
Deary me, that sounds like a porn film.
(Mind you, I'd watch it.)

Moon. Simon. Simon. Moon.

I spent a night of passion with a particle physicist,
And we danced under the stars.
And we held each other tight.
In the absolute oneness of our romance,

I asked her what she thought of the Simon.
She slapped me.

Moon. Simon. Simon. Moon.

Simon is the size of Australia,
Except it's spherical, which Australia isn't.
It's got a B-side.
It's got a B-side.
A dark side.
Simon's got a dark side.
If Australia had a dark side,
They'd probably fill it up with
More of those fiddly marsupials.

Moon. Simon. Simon. Moon.

Dave says the Milky Way is slightly moist.
Dave says Venus is shaped like a duck.
Dave says Jupiter is fluffy
And it was probed in the 1970s.
I often take heed of Dave's knowledge
Though he reckons he was
Also probed in the 1970s.
Dave's a bit weird sometimes.

Moon. Simon. Simon. Moon.

I was floating through the universe the other day
Like a dolphin in Primark.
The airless vacuum made my hair all frizzy.
As I re-entered the atmosphere
I brushed the surface of Simon.

Moon. Simon. Simon. Moon.

The moon should wear a wig.
That will jazz it up a bit.
Nothing too flash,

But something to conceal its baldness.
We'll work on its craters
Laters.

Moon. Simon. Simon. Moon.

I bound across your surface
Like an astronaut with a bus to catch.
Bouncy bouncy bouncy.
Flump flump flump.
I bound across your surface
Like a potato rolling down the stairs.
Bouncy bouncy bouncy.
Plop plop plop.

Moon. Simon. Simon. Moon.

Simon, Simon, in the night sky.
I often wonder why,
When night clouds drift by,
You throw down your lunar glow,
Throw down your lunar glow,
But to the earth it doesn't go,
Because of all those clouds
That I just mentioned.
Did you switch off the light, Moon Simon?
Click, click, off.

Moon. Simon. Simon. Moon.

The moon isn't really made of cheese.
Otherwise Apollo 11 would have brought back a sandwich.
The lunar module was called the Eagle
But its occupants nicknamed it 'Timothy'.
Neil Armstrong wasn't the first man on the moon.
It was the cameraman.
I saw a documentary about methods of attaching panels to ships.
It was riveting.

I put my name down for origami classes.
But they folded.
The surface of the moon is barren
And lacking in atmosphere.
Newton Abbot.
The moon isn't always called Simon.
On its birthday it's called Mr Plumbridge.
On its birthday it's called Mr Plumbridge.
On its birthday it's called Mr Plumbridge.
On its birthday it's called Mr Plumbridge.

Moon. Simon. Simon. Moon.

Fishy fishy sparkle sparkle,
Swim fish swim.
Fishy fishy sparkle sparkle,
The sun is also called Jim.

Moon. Simon. Simon. Moon.
Moon. Simon. Simon. Moon.
Simon. Moon. Simon.
Simon. Moon. Simon. Simon.
Moon. Simon. Simon. Moon.

POEM

I spent a night of passion with Flozzie Bear
From the *Fluppet Show*.
The whole encounter was surprisingly erotic.
At sensitive and pleasurable moments he had a habit
Of suddenly shouting, 'Wacka wacka wacka,'
Which kind of took the shine off things.
He kept his hat on all the time.
He marked out his territory all over the living room.
He mauled the postman.
He was a surprisingly good kisser.

We chatted about philosophy and he told me his belief
That he was being controlled at all times
By unseen hands.
I told him my Uncle Sid owned a trilby the same as his.
Flozzie asked if Uncle Sid was a Fluppet and I said no,
He worked for the gas board.
And then Flozzie said, 'You know those two old men?
Those two old men who used to heckle me all the time?
Do you remember them?
All that heckling they did?
They're dead now, the pair of them.
Dead and buried.'
'So,' I said, 'you had the last laugh.'
'Not really,' he replied. 'You should see
The abuse I get on Twitter.'
I changed the subject back to Uncle Sid.

With the lights off he became tender and loving.
He ran his fluffy fingers through my hair
And told me that he'd not felt like this
Since a failed romance with the Norwegian Chef.
He took off his polka-dot bow tie
And knotted it round my wrist.
I found it strangely erotic.
'Do you want to wear the hat?' he asked.
'No, thanks,' I replied,
Put off by sudden visions of Uncle Sid.

'Wear it,' he said. 'Wear it.
Wear it.
Wear the hat.
Go on.
Put the hat on.
Put the hat on.
Put it on.
Wear it.
I want you to wear the hat.
I want you to wear the hat.
I want you to wear the hat.
Put the hat on.
Put it on, bad boy.
Wear it, bad boy.
Wear it, stud muffin.
Wear it, you tart.
Wear it, you tart.
Wear the hat wear the hat wear the hat
Just wear the bloody hat!'
I put it on and he wacka wacka wacka-ed.

He left before the night was over.
He stole my wallet.

POEM

Glass flan dishes
From Cuba.

Baking dishes
From Antigua.

Quiche dishes
From the Yucatan Peninsula.

Measuring jugs
From the West Indies.

Microwave-proof glass pans
From Trinidad.

Yes, it's the
Pyrex of the Caribbean.

POEM

When Steven dumped me
I bought a microwave oven.
When James dumped me
I bought a new kettle.
When Darren dumped me
I bought a new kettle
(Because the last one had stopped working).
When Andrew dumped me
I bought a toaster.
When Philip dumped me
I bought an ironing board.
When Paul dumped me
I bought a coffee machine.
It's been a hell of a week.

POEM

I've just taken up baton-twirling.
It's all spandex and lip gloss,
But I've mastered the fundamentals.
I'm pretty good at it.
The only problem is that I haven't got a baton.
But I do have an eel called Bridget.

She likes being flung up in the air
But from the outside it looks pretty disgusting.
'Stay rigid,' I keep telling her. 'Stay rigid,
Bridget.'
She doesn't half moan when I drop her.
I tell her not to fidget,
Bridget.
'Come on, Bridget,' I whisper.
I fling her around
But only seldom have I missed her.
Once we practised all day
And I got a blister.
Once we did so well
That I very nearly kissed her.
The crowd felt quite ill
Watching me trying to snog an eel.

We came dead last.
We certainly had a blast.
And the atmosphere was electric,
Unlike Bridget, who's just a regular eel.

POEM

Unrolling a new bin liner.
I haven't found the
Perforations yet.

Unrolling, unrolling, unrolling.
How much more can there be?

Unrolling, unrolling, unrolling.
This simple act becomes
An existentialist conundrum.
What else in life
Have I been doing so wrong?
Do I always go charging ahead
And forget the present moment?
Perhaps I have already passed
The perforations,
And didn't notice.

Perhaps it hasn't even got
Perforations.

Perhaps everything I've done in my life
Has been but a mirage, a forgery,
And a fake.

Unrolling, unrolling, unrolling.
Unrolling, unrolling, unrolling.
Unrolling.
Found them.

POEM

I'm being kept awake by my neighbours,
By the total lack of any evidence
Of them ever having sex.

It's most perplexing.
The nights pass in a silence so deep
As to be almost unnatural,
That a couple so virile and so seemingly
Up For It and Massively In Love
As they
Should spend their nights
Doing something other
Than being one another's lover.

Whatever it is they're doing
Is nothing like screwing,
And very quiet.
Stolen kisses, perhaps,
Quiet moans,
Perhaps they wait for when
I'm not at home.

I lie in my bed at night,
I cannot sleep,
My heart it yearns.
Perhaps they take turns.

Occasionally they make noises
Of a sort, as we all do,
Creaking floorboards
And a flushing loo.
But there's something they lack
Once they get in the sack.

No grunts, no groans,
No whispered moans,
No laughter, no giggle,
No slap and tickle,
I hear no joy, no energy,

No enthusiasm,
Unless they've developed
The World's Quietest Orgasm.

I'm starting to become obsessed
By what they're not doing.
I'm thinking of suing.
I'm up till three in the morning,
Then four,
Because of all the silence next door,
Wondering if their dirty talk
Is conducted in semaphore,
Pondering and speculating
Over their silent ejaculating.
If they're being amorous,
It's hardly clamorous,
And I'm lying there,
Wondering if they're dying there,
Because it sounds exactly like this:

'

                    .'

There must be a reason why
He's never kissed her.
Perhaps she's his sister.

POEM

An ocelot isn't a badger.
It's a *not-badger*.
A prairie dog isn't a badger.
It's also a *not-badger*.
An elephant isn't a badger.
Obvs.
It's an elephant.
Any fool can see that,
What with its tusks.
My dental hygienist isn't a badger.
She, again, is a *not-badger*.

Therefore the ocelot, the prairie dog,
The elephant and my dental hygienist
Are all, similarly, *not-badgers*.

They are the same in the full
Semantic morphological normative scope
Of rational thought
And are as distinct from a badger
As a Citroën or a kettle.

In essence, therefore,
They are the same.

If a man one day from Mars
Landed and saw the ocelot,
The prairie dog, the elephant
And my dental hygienist,
He'd think,
They're all
Earthlings.

But if he saw a badger
He'd probably think,
Hey, it's Kevin,
I think I shall
Buy him an ice cream.

POEM

We entrusted in you such quips as to colour
Our humdrum
As you were different and mildly
Entertaining.
I chuckled, certainly,
Pleasantly surprised at what I first
Mistook for whimsy,
Only later to be revealed
As the toxic utterances of an attention-seeking
Knobhead.
That's why I call this poem
'The rise and fall of Jeremy Clarkson'.

Oh you saggy-bottomed baggy-jowelled
Loud-mouthed red-faced cretin,
With an expression like a spinster aunt
Straining out a poo in the station toilet
Three minutes before her train is due.
How you so desperately exploit the idea
That it's not words that make a man
But the tone of your voice.
Volume doesn't make you right.
How many PE teachers have also been
World-class philosophers?*

But it has made you very rich.
How you soared, like a belching eagle,
Like a phoenix with fat jokes,
Like a pterodactyl with piles,
Grabbing at chance and finding
Those two other knobheads,
The one who obviously adores you,
And the one who obviously can't stand you
And is only in it for the money.
He reminds me of my ex.

----
* I forgot about Albert Camus.

You don't need brains to drive a car,
Just a modicum of common sense
And a feel for the bite of the clutch.
You don't need brains to watch *Top Gear*,
Just a hint of righteous indignation
And the last simpering gasp
Of blokey matishness
Where the ultimate insult is to have it hinted
On national television that
You might not be entirely heterosexual.
You know what they say about
Men with big cars.

It means they've got small knobs.
I thought I'd spell it out for you.

I bought some cheese the other day.
It told me not to go out in the rain
And to save my money.
It was a very mature cheddar.

You're sinking now, Clarky.
You're like the Titanic in reverse
In that the only tragedy was that
You managed to stay afloat for so long.
You're sinking now, revealed to a world
That thought you were funny
That you're nothing but a great big tit
With, as I said before, a little willy.

Oh, Clarkson, you drivelling snotbag,
You automotive weasel pea-brained rapscallion,
You bulbous-eyed odious
Clay-brained stench, you crusty scab
On the face of common decency,
You rhetorical amalgam of petrol-inhaling obviousness,
You oily-jeaned spongy-thighed unnecessary
Foul-brained ass of a man,

How I long for you to be photographed
Making love to a Ford Focus while
Your co-hosts wank in the corner,
How I long for that,
How I long for that day!

Drive the car, Clarkson.
Drive it, drive the car,
Ram it into gear and drive that car.
Let me lick the side
Of your big craggy face.

POEM

He said my cat was *'kind of camp'*.
I said, 'How can it be camp?
It has no sense either of postmodernist irony
Or the subtle sexual politics of attraction,
Signification, semantics,
And all those other processes.'
'I don't know,' he said,
'But your cat is kind of camp.

'It wears a little sailor's hat,
And it minces when it walks,
And when it meows it sounds like
Kenneth Williams.
When it laps milk from a dish
It then pads its mouth with a lace napkin
Which it holds out for someone to take.'

'That's not camp,' I replied,
'That's just good breeding.'

'It makes,' he said,
'Elaborate gestures with its paws.
And it knows all the show tunes.
And it doesn't eat mice because
It says they're fattening.
And it's always tidying up.
And it's obsessed with celebrity culture,
Ogling over pictures of what the cat
From the opening titles of *Coronation Street*
Is up to these days.
And that's why I think
That your cat
Is kind of camp.'

I thought about his insinuations.
I found them a little scary.
Did they hide a latent homophobia?
And why was it his business to ask?

What assumptions can he make
Without diving into someone's mind?

That night, in the back yard,
I called for my cat.
'Justin.
Justin.
Justin.
Oh, Justin.
Justin.
Justin.
Justin.
Where are you, Justin?'

Justin came mincing out of the rhododendrons
And gave me that kind of withering,
Supercilious stare,
Threw the end of his feather boa around his neck
And started eating his quiche.

POEM

A friend of mine thinks he might be
Straight.
I told him, 'There's a lot of it going around.
Someone's got to be watching all this football on TV.
And I thought something was amiss
The moment you started wearing polyester
Sports-themed leisure-wear
And eating McCoy's crisps.
And building sheds.
And watching *Top Gear*.
And saying things like
Phwoarr, look at the size of those bahzooms!

'It's nothing to be ashamed of.
Some of the most exciting people around at the moment
Are straight.
Like Richard Madeley,
And Wayne Rooney,
And Andy Murray,
And Peter Andre,
And Alan Titchmarsh,
And Nick Clegg.'

I told him,
'Now look, Andrew.
You baulk at quiche.
You read *The Sun*.
And when you tell an interesting anecdote
You always start at the end and work your way to the
beginning.
You watched *Titanic* and laughed when the boat sank.
You went into Starbucks and you moaned
When they said that they didn't do chips.
I think you might be straight.

'You laugh at the hairstyles of the presenters
On *The Culture Show*.
You watch *Hollyoaks*

And you kind of shift upwards in your seat a little bit
When one of the women in it
Looks like she might take her top off.
But they never do.
You know what a crankshaft is and what it does
But you never laugh when anyone says "crankshaft".
I think you might be straight.

'But it doesn't change a thing.
In spite of your straightness,
It doesn't change a thing.
In spite of your level barking,
Ever so heartening,
Masculine muscle-crunched fish-'n'-chip lunched,
Deep fat-fried hair – not blow-dried,
Never walked in Gay Pride,
Oily-handed sports-theme-branded
Straighty matey farting belching
Darts-playing wood-sawing boob-gawping
Cable-lagging dreams-of-Kylie-shagging
Straitjacketing straight-talking straight-living
Straight-shooting straighty straighty straight
Life to which you have plummeted to such effect as to seem
Almost ironic, as to appear
'Just
A
Little
Camp.

'I think on reflection you may be
On the most part
Rampantly heterosexual,
If it weren't for what we got up to last night.'

POEM

Helen's got an X-ray goat.
It's just like a normal goat
But with X-ray vision,
Or so Helen said.
She keeps it in a shed
To protect the modesty of the
Other goats,
Some of whom object
To its X-ray vision.

I asked Helen
How she came about
This goat with supernatural powers.
She said she found it in a field
Looking at a horse,
Strangely.
And later it turned out
That the horse had eaten a flip-flop.

'What are you going to do,
What are you going to do,
What are you going to do
With an X-ray goat?' I asked.
And Helen beamed that famous grin
And said she was hiring it out
To Bristol Airport
In order to search for bombs.
I asked what it would do
If it found a bomb
And she said,
'Probably run like hell.'

'It also shoots lasers
Out of its horns,' she said.
'Last Thursday it ignited a barn.
I had to remove the combine harvester
And two roosters.'

That night we made sweet love
But I was put off by the X-ray goat
Glaring up at the bedroom
All night long from the yard.
Just staring up, staring up, staring up
At the bedroom.
'It does that,' she sighed.

POEM

Orgasms.
I've heard they're pretty good.
People seem to like them.
I thought I had one once.
It was a Thursday.

Orgasms.
My Aunt Phyllis swears by them.

Orgasms.
All that hard work has to be rewarded
With something.
It's like putting up a garden shed
And being given a cup of tea,
Except the next time you go round
The shed's gone
And they've lost the kettle.

Orgasms.
My friend Luke likes to have them
In his car.
It's like the ultimate blend of man and woman and machine,
He says, so long as you've still got a hand free
To change gear.

Orgasms.
I faked my last three.
But that's what happens
When you live on your own
And you've got washing-up to get on with.

Orgasms.
It's like that feeling you get
When the bus finally turns up
Only probably twice as good.

Orgasms.
It's like waiting for the toaster
And then you realise that
The kitchen is on fire.

Orgasms.
Moustache quivering.

Orgasms.
Not always compulsory.

Orgasms.
Like a bourbon biscuit
On a plate
With the frilly doily.

Orgasms.
Almost onomatopoeic.

Orgasms.
A split second of bliss,
Bit of a bummer if the phone rings.

Orgasms.
Kind of puts you off to think
That Terry Wogan has probably had them.

Orgasms.
It's like tidying up before going out
And coming back
And forgetting you've tidied
And opening the front door and thinking,
Gosh, it looks tidy in here.

Orgasms.
Like that feeling you get
When you've written a really good line of poetry
Which I didn't get
While working on this one.
Or this one.
Or this one.

Orgasms.
They're like plane crashes
In that they don't seem to happen

As often as they used to
But when they do
There's a hell of a mess
And then an intense investigation.

Orgasms.
A sneeze is one third of one.
I'm allergic to fur.
I've been hanging round the cattery
With a box of tissues and a tin of Whiskas.

Orgasms.
Feel the heat rush,
The tingly bliss,
A sudden release from the tyranny
Of normal sensation
The exquisite juddering shuddering
Heart-tickling moment-splitting absolute
Palpitation-thumping dear God
Where's that coming from?
Draw the curtains, Mavis,
They're at it again
Oh my this is most pleasant
Split second of awful hideous
Resplendent ecstasy
I mean
I mean
I've read about them
And they do sound rather enjoyable.

POEM

I've always wanted a beard,
Just never had the time to grow one.
Whenever I see them I get this
Strange feeling inside
Of deep inadequacy.

I want a beard like Jonathan's got.
I like the cut of his jib.
Beardy beardy man, how lucky you are.
Chinny chin chin keeps tickling while kissing
I expect.

I went to the barber and I said,
'Give me a beard, good man,
And make it a big bushy one like I'm an
Old grizzled trawlerman.
Here's a Pritt Stick, now sweep up the floor
And stick it on my chin, there's a good fellow.'
It fell off
When I was halfway round Lidl's.

Last night I sat in envy
At the annual Beard Slam.
It was won by a geography teacher
Whose beard looked like
Two ferret-shaped sideburns mating
While a badger-shaped moustache
Hid in the rhododendrons and took photos.

I saw a man in the pub with a beard
And his friend had a beard
And his wife had a beard
And their dog had a beard
And the barman had a beard
And the barman said, through his beard,
'What would you like?' and I said,
'A beard,'
And the barman said I was weird,
So I ordered an Apple and Raspberry J2O.

I can't look at a goat!
I hate the way they gloat!
With their nanny goat billy goat beard beard
Unwarranted goatee goatee sprout sprout
Stroke it,
Stroke it, big boy!

I went to the circus and I saw a beard tamer
Cracking his whip
Beard tamer
Cracking his whip
Beard tamer
Pass me the shaver!
Stay there, boy.
Stay there, boy.
Cutting them down into
Very
Very
Very
Very
Very
Long
Sideburns.

If I had a beard I'd
Dip the end in chocolate sauce
And draw crazy patterns on your smooth
Bare chest whispering, 'Growl for me,
Growl for your lover man, growl like a tiger,
You sexed-up beast of a man!'
Which would probably startle
The other people on the bus.

I want to grow a beard so big
It might have to be bioengineered!

Fuzzy fuzzy chin scratch
Scrunch up

Feel it
Feel it
Go on
Put your hand here and feel it.
Arghhhhhh!

POEM

The first time I had sex I remember thinking,
This is not the sort of thing that usually happens to me.
How right I was.

It put me in mind of a thirteenth-century jousting tournament
And it gave me a nosebleed.

The person I was doing it at
Was very patient.
Very very patient.
Very very very very very very patient.
'Don't worry,' he said,
'It happens, sometimes.'
How right he was.

I remember undressing
And his complexion changed
And a frown overtook his features.
'What is it?' I asked.
'I've just remembered,' he replied,
'I've got to go out tomorrow and buy some
Extra extra extra small bite-sized sausages.'

'The anticipation,' he said,
'Makes it all the more sweet,
And I know you wanted to try some foreplay,
But please, can we not have another game of Buckaroo
And just go to bed?'

We decided to incorporate some food.
He squirted cream on my chest
And gently licked it off.
And I did the same to him
With a pizza and some garlic bread

And a selection of potato wedges
Washed down with a large Pepsi cola.

'That's good,' he said.
'That's very good.
Oh, that's so good.
Oh, I hope it never stops,' he said.
'That's so so good.
Oh my, that really is most absolutely fantastic.
Oh. That's good.
Oh yes.
Oh yes indeed.
Oh, mamma. That's the best cup of tea
I've had in a long while.'

He lit some candles and called it 'mood lighting'.
I watched the moths circle, endlessly.
I closed my eyes
And tried to think about someone else.
For some reason the only person who sprang to mind
Was German Chancellor Angela Merkel.

Just after midnight I really started
Getting into the swing of it.
I let the outside world dissipate
As I found a sweet rhythm.
The sensual glide of time on fate,
Bodies sliding with their own
Inexorable rhythms
As the pounding whisper of oneness
Finally began to seem in reach
And I went for it
And I ground out my love
And I went for it
Feeling everything combine
In the actual sensual beautiful
Exquisitely awful ecstatic
Spasmodic sheer sheer bliss of it all
Interrupted only when he said,
'Hey, hey, I'm over here,
In the kitchen.'

POEM

Jake's sturdy upper body
Has been replaced by a bark-covered
Trunk.
And his arms are gone, substituted
With branches which
Silhouette against the sky.
And his head is now a canopy,
Wearing leaves instead of a baseball cap,
And he's grown from a relatively stumpy
Five-foot-five
To a whopping thirty-eight metres.
And instead of walking around
He mostly just stays in the one place.
And instead of eating burgers
He indulges in photosynthesis.
And instead of moaning about things
He creaks in the breeze.

On Wednesday I asked him if he could
Help move a chest of drawers
And he said he couldn't
Because it looked like it was made
From his Uncle George.

POEM

The new fridge-freezer
Is suspiciously quiet.
Erik said it would make a humming noise.

Put some apples in there.
Put some yoghurt in there.
It's still just as quiet.

It sucks life out of the obvious.
My friend Nadine bought a new fridge-freezer
And hers was suspiciously quiet
And then it exploded.

Put some feta cheese in there.
Put some Laughing Cow in there.
Hum, damn you, hum.

Not even a self-satisfied hum
Or a hum of annoyance,
Just a hum.

Nervous glances from the kitchen door.
I can't sleep with that thing in the house.
Three in the morning, pacing up and down.
Nervous, nervous, nervous in the kitchen.

I phone up Erik
And ask about the humming
And he enquires as to whether
It is actually a wardrobe.

POEM

A lorry full of paperclips
Broke down on the motorway.
Ground to a trundling halt.
Stationery.

POEM

I don't think I exist.
By not thinking I exist,
I am at least thinking,
And therefore this proves
That I exist,
Which is not what I think.

POEM

I saw the monotone poet
Gesticulating
And I went to acknowledge his gesture
Unaware
That he was not waving
But droning.

POEM

I wish I had a pound
For every time I'd made love.

Oh, the fun I'd have wondering
How I'd spend that £38.

I could buy six cushions,
Or I could buy a new kettle,
Or I could buy
Thirty-eight tubes of Pringles crisps.

And these I would place
In a circle, the circumference of which
Would be like a mini-Stonehenge
Celebrating those sacred thirty-eight occasions
On which I'd made love.

Oh, that wonderful blend of the
Sweet and the sour, terribly salty,
Bad for you, yet oh, so moreish,
Leading ultimately to a rampant
Stomach ache and hours of deep regret.
But the crisps were nice.

Every time I'd eat a cheese and onion flavour,
I'd think of Jamie.
Every time I'd eat a beef flavour,
I'd think of Aaron.
Every time I'd have the plain flavour,
I'd think of Darren
Because Darren was oh so plain
And afterwards he said that our love
Had just been a consequence of circumstance
Mixed with a touch of alcohol
Plus most of it went on the carpet.

He's got a point.
It probably doesn't count.
Which means I'm down to thirty-seven.

POEM

There once was a man from Aberystwyth
Who was an existentialist.
While eating some ham
He said, 'I am.'

POEM

I wrote a letter to Buzz Aldrin.
It started,
'All right, Buzz?
Second on the moon, eh?
All that preparation
And the hopes and the dreams
And you're forever remembered
As the Also Man,
The Also-Ran,
Stepping out second from
A spaceship tin can.
I once came second in a
Flower-arranging contest,
So I know how it feels.

'And your friends,
They never stop their joshing.
I hear you've got a cartoon
On your wall, depicting a signpost
On the moon
Which reads, "Buzz Stop".

'Second on the moon.
Did you get a buzz, Buzz?
Or were you looking at Armstrong thinking,
You absolute sodding bastard?
You should have dropped your anguish
And raised your fists. Settled it like gentlemen
Bundling in the lunar module.
You're two hundred and forty thousand
Miles from home, Mr Aldrin.
No chance of calling the fuzz, Buzz.

'You should have made one giant leap
And kicked him in the goolies!

'Oh, Buzz.
Buzz Buzz Buzz.

I think of you every time
I use my
Vibrator.

'My mum always compares your exploits
With other things.
"We can send a man to the moon," she says,
"And yet still not design a yoghurt which doesn't
Squirt everywhere the moment you open it."
"It's not the same," I tell her.
"It's not the same."
But then she gets all philosophical and says,
"Advancement is in the minor details."
It's hard to imagine
That she's also said things like,
"I'd give my right arm to be ambidextrous."

'Anyway, Buzz.
I look at what you've achieved
And I apply it to my own life.
I've never been to the moon
But I've been to Newton Abbot,
And it's similarly desolate and lifeless.

I've been to parties that were
Lacking in atmosphere
And I've followed in the footsteps
Of those who achieved historic greatness
Like that time I shared an elevator
With Dale Winton.

'I've bounded across the surface
Of foreign bodies
Like that time I spent
A night of passion with
A Lithuanian.
And I've sensed the excitement
Of a ticker-tape parade

When that kid in the tower block
Threw a toilet roll at me.
And I may not have been in orbit,
But I once accidentally drove
Twice round the Norwich ring road.

'Buzz.
I often think of you, Buzz.
When I'm sitting on the bus, Buzz.
Whenever I see a bumblebee, Buzz.
Whenever I reach out for the infinite
And someone else gets there just a
Fraction of a second before me,
Like that time another customer got the
Last Müller Corner yoghurt in the supermarket
Before me,
Buzz.

Whenever I pour a cup of tea
And realise I hadn't boiled the kettle, Buzz.
You are my talisman, Buzz.
My reason for being, Buzz.
You showed me how to live, Buzz.
You showed me that it's not what
You did or what you've done, Buzz,
But what you does, Buzz.

'Yours sincerely, Robert Garnham.
P.S. Please find enclosed your Tesco Clubcard statement.'

POEM

Your eyes are the most perfect eyes ever,
Like deep blue swimming pools, beautifully oval,
Repeated, surrounded by Mediterranean bleached whitewash,
Intense, loving, focussed.

Your mouth is delicate and the most perfect mouth ever,
Like sculptory, finely caressed,
Like the hint of a pout that makes you look twice
Just to confirm that there isn't a pout.

Your nose is the most perfect nose ever,
Slender and proportioned with the tiniest upwards step,
Architectural, non-obtrusive, tapering
With really nice nostrils.

Your earlobes are all right.

Your chin is the most perfect chin ever,
Neither jutting nor insistent, yet sculpted,
Tentative, smooth, with a little dimple in the middle
Yet not one of those big chins that you sometimes see.

Your chest is wide and the most perfect chest ever,
Smooth, like warm ice, like heaven,
Like an invitation, a slide,
Like the newly resurfaced carriageway
Between Honiton and Exeter.

Your molecules are the most perfect molecules ever.
I'd spend eternity just counting them.
One, two, three, four, five, six, seven, eight, is how I'd start,
Nine, ten, eleven, etc. etc., you've got lots of them.

Your eyebrows are the most perfect eyebrows ever,
Neither rampant nor obvious, yet finely drawn
With perfect equidistance between eyes and forehead
So as to draw attention
To your forehead
Which is also the most perfect
Forehead ever.

Your spleen is
Well, to be honest, I
Don't know much about your spleen.

Your eyelashes are the most perfect eyelashes ever,
Slyly arced in a parabola of beauty,
Fluttering and aerodynamic, beauteous blinkers,
Interlocking momentarily like brackets
Enclosing the word *orgasm*.

Your rosy cheeks are the most perfect rosy cheeks ever
(To be honest,
This verse is a bit boring,
So I've left the rest of it out).

Your hair is the most perfect hair ever,
Blond and fine and perfectly obedient
Like an ornate frame on a Flemish masterpiece,
Knowingly fashionable, and yet, as if by accident, divine.

Your mind is the most perfect mind ever,
Like a computer, like a processor, like a machine,
Like a chance, like a dream, like a repository of
Things which are never as they seem, oh how I scream
To ponder on the things that I've seen and the thought that
You don't know just what this longing means.

And your frontal lobes are top-notch.

You are so very perfect, the most perfect person ever,
With your perfect life
And your perfect aspirations
And your perfect dress sense and your perfect manners
Which create a perfect barrier keeping out all slight tiny
Ingratiating imperfections.
If only you'd notice me from time to time,
But until then
I shall use someone else's
Till
At the supermarket.

POEM

When I was six
And my sister was four
She once freaked out
Because she got cuckoo spit on her hand.

My parents tried to calm her
Yet no amount of saying,
'Don't worry, it's only cuckoo spit,'
Seemed to do the job.

It's a common misconception
That cuckoo spit comes from cuckoos.
It's actually the foamy phlegm
Of an insect called the froghopper,
More commonly known in some quarters
As the 'flob beetle'.

'Don't be so frantic, Angela,
Don't be so frantic!
It's only the regurgitated foam
Of a froghopper.
Nothing to worry about!'

Weren't you always like this?

Freaking out over the small things.
Going off on one over fripperies,
Your suburban mindset already set out
At age four suddenly brought back to Earth
By spit from an insect.
Don't be so frantic, Angela,
Don't be so frantic.

The froghopper encases itself in phlegm,
Which provides warmth and nutrition
And helps to attract a female.
The bigger the wodge of spit,
The more rampant and fertile the male.
You should hear them at night

During mating season.
You can't sleep for the sound of

One thousand spittle bugs hawking back
Rhythmically
As much spit as they can muster
Hoping to attract a female
By the impressive amount they can gob.
You can't get to sleep.
It's really quite disgusting.

Don't be so frantic, Angela,
Don't be so frantic.
It's only the hopeful love juices
Of the sexed-up male phlegm beetle.
Nothing to worry about.
Be brave, you gallant
Saliva survivor!

Cuckoo spit in the foliage,
Cuckoo spit in the undergrowth,
Cuckoo spit in the rhododendrons,
Cuckoo spit on my sister's hand.
Watch her leading off now,
Screaming and yelling and
Blaming me for some reason.
Jeez, she was so melodramatic
For a four-year-old.

Cuckoo spit in the bushes,
Cuckoo spit in the shrubbery.
My sister yelling and some poor
Flob beetle somewhere
Suddenly far less attractive to the
Female of his species.
He's not going to get his leg over
Tonight
And it's all my sister's fault.

SNOW WHITE AND THE
SEVEN COFFEE TABLES

Snow White trailed her delicate fingers along
The coffee table surface
Thinking, *What the hell am I going to do with all these?*
I don't even drink coffee.
So you can see the bind I'm in.

When the order was received for a sixth coffee table,
Most people thought there had been an administrative error.
When an order came through for a seventh,
It was generally assumed that something was amiss.

At nights, Snow White places a Bakewell tart
On each freshly-polished coffee table.
And you know what?
Then she goes around the room and she eats the lot.
I don't know how she keeps her figure.

She was heard to say one day to an advisor,
'I keep stumbling from one disaster to the next,
Stumbling and bumbling.
Must be all the coffee tables.

'I keep banging my shins.'

'Mirror, mirror, on the wall,
Who's the prettiest of them all?'
'You are, my dear,' the mirror replies,
'In spite of all those unsightly bruises
On your shins.'

POEM

I wrote the names of the seven dwarves
One each on seventeen paper lanterns.
Only afterwards did I realise
I'd discovered ten extra.

I tried to jump to catch the lanterns
To verify my discovery
But they flew up and away and I couldn't reach.
I think one of them had been called Neil.

Now I spend my nights bereft
Trying to remember the names I'd written.
Tomorrow I shall go out and buy
Seventeen more lanterns.

Perhaps (and I'm only guessing this),
I just made it all up.
But I can never be too sure.
These things just seem to happen.

POEM

He's got a T-shirt
Showing a duck in a tutu.
He's got a T-shirt
Showing a badger at a DJ's mixing desk.
He's got a T-shirt
Showing *Star Trek*'s Jean-Luc Picard doing
The washing-up.
He's got a T-shirt
With the word Geek on it.
So he must be a Geek.
That's the inference.
He's buying in to the whole *Geek* ethos
By wearing a T-shirt with the word
Geek on it.
He should have a T-shirt which reads
I am a tosser.
That would probably be more apt.

He's got a T-shirt
With a picture of Private Sponge
From *Dad's Army* on it.
You're so clever, aren't you?
Showing all the world that you know
Who Private Sponge from *Dad's Army* is.
That's a great popular culture reference there.
You must be so witty.
I want to hang around with you.
Let's go and play snooker some time,
You know,
Ironically.
Perhaps some of your wittiness
Will rub off on me.

He's got a T-shirt
With *Ree* on one side
And *Bok* on the other.
He went to Turkey once
And didn't realise

That *Bok* is an incredibly filthy word
In Turkey.
What a knob.

He's got a T-shirt
With a picture of Tenby on it
And the words *Beautiful Tenby*
That his aunt bought him from Tenby.
He wears it ironically.
Not all of his friends get it.
Nathan thinks that he just really likes Tenby.

He's got a T-shirt
With the cast of *Family Guy* on it.
He's got a T-shirt
With those idiots from *Top Gear* on it.
He's got a T-shirt
With the Two Ronnies on it.
He doesn't know who the Two Ronnies are.
He thinks they're Morecambe and Wise.

He's got a T-shirt
From Ashburton Owl Sanctuary.
He's got a T-shirt
Celebrating Liverpool winning the cup.
It's quite an old one.
He's got a T-shirt that says,
I'm a flat-packed wardrobe. Join me.
He's got a T-shirt that says,
Official Boob Inspector,
Form a queue.
He's got a T-shirt
That says,
Cover me in chocolate
And throw me to the lesbians.
That's
Cover me in chocolate
And throw me to the lesbians.

He's got a T-shirt which says,
I'm an atheist, goddammit.
He doesn't get it.

In fact, he's got
Lots of T-shirts.
Only when you actually come
To speak to him
He never has anything interesting
To say.
He comes from Guildford.

POEM

There's a blue whale
In the library.
It's clear it's in a place
It's not meant to be.

No one knows
How it got
Through the door.
Now there's blubber
All over the floor.

Marjorie the librarian
Lost her date stamp
Down the blowhole.

POEM

Don't you come at me with your hydrangea shit
'Cause once you've seen a fuchsia then you know
You've been hit.
Its flowers are prettier than a girl who's quite fit
And they're hardy annuals too so they last for a bit.

I'm a hard-ass gun and I don't feel no pain
Like the petals of the fuchsia in the early evening rain,
Like the same old song you hear again and again,
My roots don't go rotten if the compost's well drained.

So dig up that fuchsia, man, dig up that fuchsia,
'Cause you and me, honey, we ain't got no future.
Dig up that fuchsia, girl, put it in a pot,
'Cause when I'm here with you, girl, I feel I lost the plot.

I'm a kicking mother sparkler and I know how to party,
Coming at you with the beats and a bottle of Bacardi.
I don't feel no cold 'cause I'm mostly frost hardy
So when you're out and you're chilling
Then you gotta wear a cardy.

I'm a fit fat hip-hop sexy damn mo-fo
Hanging at my pad with my bitches and my hoes
And my trowels and my rakes and my petrol-driven lawn mow.
A big bag of mulch and some compost make me grow, yo.

So dig up that fuchsia, man, dig up that fuchsia,
'Cause you and me, honey, we ain't got no future.
Dig up that fuchsia, girl, chuck it on the bonfire,
'Cause when I'm here with you, girl, I feel my heart is on fire.

When I see you coming, girl, you light up the room
Like a late summer fuchsia as it comes into bloom
With its delicate petals, you make my heart boom
And not only that but I really like your bahzooms.

In a world filled with pain and with hatred and with greed
I'm a delicate flower, not a dirty stinking weed

'Cause I've felt this ache inside since I was a little seed.
I'm a funky mother fuchsia and I get what I need.

So dig up that fuchsia, man, dig up that fuchsia,
'Cause you and me, honey, we ain't got no future.
Dig up that fuchsia, girl, rip it out that border bed,
'Cause when I'm here with you, girl, I'd rather be in your bed.

I got delicate petals in the hue of summer fruit
And a purposeful demeanour from my sternum to my root
But when I look at you, girl, you really are so cute.
Like the homies in my hood, you gotta be my side shoot.

When I'm here with you, girl, I never question why,
I just sit here in my border bed and gaze up at the sky.
Try to weed me out, girl, I'd like to see you try.
You're more irritating than a nasty case of greenfly.

So dig up that fuchsia, man, dig up that fuchsia,
'Cause you and me, honey, we ain't got no future.
Dig up that fuchsia, girl, put it in a pot,
'Cause when I'm here with you, girl, I feel I lost the plot.

You can make my heart sing, can you hear it crooning?
Like that feeling that I get from a really good pruning.
The world is so bright, with nothing that can spoil
That comfort that I feel when you become my topsoil.

You make me want to scream and shout, temper my sobriety,
Make me become a member of the Horticultural Society.
My friends they are so jealous, you should see them glower so,
A big gold trophy from your first place at the flower show.

So dig up that fuchsia, man, dig up that fuchsia,
'Cause you and me, honey, we ain't got no future.
Dig up that fuchsia, girl, you should hear my heart weep,
My hopes and dreams lying face-down on the compost heap.

POEM

I always seem to associate
Several Surrey towns
With shades of beige as marketed
By the Ford Motor Company in the 1970s.

Egham is Nevada beige.
Woking is Sahara beige.
Weybridge is classic cream beige.
Guildford is light beige.
Staines is antique beige.

I know Staines has a Middlesex postal address
But it's definitely in Surrey.

My friend Steven opines
That I always get excitable
And blunder on through life
And he might have a point.

I like the display of busts
In one of the galleries at the British Museum.
I can't remember which gallery it is
But they've all got big sideburns
And the sun slants oblong like solid dust.
I put my hand in the dust slant solid beam.
Haslemere is Bahama beige.
Horsell is Toucan beige.
Bracknell is in Berkshire but it's milk caramel beige.

In 1995 I had a bad cycle accident
And my nose has been this shape ever since.
I fell off my bike in Englefield Green
(Sonic beige).
Went riiiiiiiiiight over the handlebars.

I take time now and then
To slow down and savour life
And to commune with the exact platzgeist
Of a place/moment.

So up yours, Steven.
See, I can do it sometimes.

At nights the trains used to spark electric and
Light up the skies,
Silhouetting
Holloway College like Dracula's castle.
And I'd get ever so scared
Until,
Lulled to sleep by the friendly roar
Of transcontinental jets,
I'd dream of labyrinthine holiday cottages.

POEM

There's a professor of literature
Locked in my bathroom
And he won't come out.

Every now and then he slides
Notes under the door
Criticising the grammar
Of my medicine cabinet.
The three shelves
Remind him of haiku,
But there are more than seven pill bottles
On the middle shelf.

He unwound the toilet roll
And couldn't find a full stop.
The shower curtain
Perplexes him.

He says he can find no narrative
In the floor tiles,
Though the frosted window
Hints at more than it lets on,
Purposefully mystifying reality
Like a very fine poem
By Blake or Wordsworth
Or that Japanese chap
Who killed himself.

Last night I asked if he'd like something to eat
And he conceded that he would.
The gap underneath the door
Would only fit luncheon meat
And crisps
But he ate them nonetheless.
He admitted later on in his doctoral thesis
That he'd been very hungry.

POEM

My friend Mark has a whole room
Devoted to his trousers.
He's got two pairs of trousers.
One beige, one slightly off-beige.
They are hung in his trouser room,
Though seldom simultaneously,
As he's usually wearing his trousers,
Unless he's wearing shorts.

'Mark,' I said. 'Mark. Marky babes,
Why have you got a whole room devoted
Just to your trousers?'
And he replied that it was to stop them
From getting creased, and could I please not
Call him 'Marky babes'?

A ground-floor room, climate controlled,
Exposed oak beams, Gothic window,
Stained glass, flagstone floor,
Trousers rotating in the slightest breeze
Trousers rotating in the slightest breeze
Trousers rotating in the slightest breeze
Mesmerisingly.

In twilight the trousers take on
A personality all of their own.
The low evening sun diffused
Through stained glass captures the various
Zips, buttons and poppers
Of Mark's kecks
Like imaginary constellations decrying
Nonsensical astrology.

'Mark.
Hey, Mark.
Mark.
Mark.
Mark.

Mark.
Mark.
Hey, Mark.
Mark.
Mark.
Mark.
Mark.
Mark.
You are so devilishly impulsive.
Sorry, I thought you were Mark.'

Two years ago the local perv
Broke in and was found
Sniffing the crotch of the left-hand pair.
And since then Mark has
Always locked the door.

Mark came round the other day
And did some work for me.
I paid him with a £20 note.
He trousered it.

During the great earth tremor of 2013
They swung gently like
Two old people
At a Daniel O'Donnell concert.

There was a man in there the other day with Mark.
'Who's that?' I asked.
Mark replied,
'He's just a trouser browser.'

THE
AIR
SMELLS
FAINTLY
OF
FEBREZE

living room
kitchen
dining room
bedroom
trouser room
guest room.
He's put the house on the market.
'Why's that?' I ask.
He replies, 'I've just bought another
Pair of trousers.'

My aunt lives near Heathrow Airport
And every time a plane flies over
The glasses in her drinks cabinet
Jingle together.
(This has got nothing to do
With Mark or his trouser room.)

As a joke, as a jape, as tomfoolery,
As a cruel prank last Thursday
I let a fully grown mountain goat
Into Mark's trouser room.
But the joke was on me because
It was the local perv again
Dressed as a mountain goat.

POEM

Helen is turning into Leeds Castle.
I noticed in the sauna last night
That she's developing
R
A
Mparts.
There's a certain grey aspect to her skin.
She's got a drawbridge where before
She merely had
The normal accoutrements of a
Middle-aged lady.

Hey, Helen.
You always were impassive,
So stony-faced.
Let me clamber up your
Battlements.

Instead of a hat she's got a moat.
Instead of a handbag she's got a gift shop.
Instead of glasses she's got a keep.
Her hairstyle was a fashionable bob.
Now it's crenulated.
Instead of a coat she's got some tea rooms.

It was hot in the sauna.
She said,
'You'll get nothing out of me.'
I said,
'You're so defensive.'
She said,
'It's my job.'
I said,
'Let me get close to you.'
She said,
'I distrust all potential invaders.'
I said,
'What if I bring some ice cream?'

She said,
'One must naturally be cautious.'
I said,
'Human society is built on compromise.'
She said,
'Isn't it hot in here?'
I said,
'It's a sauna, what do you expect?'
And then a coach party of
Tourists arrived.

Oh, Helen,
I'd like to climb your
Spiral staircase
And raise my flag
From your
Immovable turrets and other
Architectural flourishes.

Ever since she started
Turning into Leeds Castle
She walks much slower
And I got frustrated in the high street
When people kept coming up and saying,
'I know you from somewhere.'

POEM

There's a tiger in the zoo
And he won't stop talking.
In fact he's quite verbose.
He's an alpha male tiger.
He's a ferocious beast.
He's called Steven.

His first words were a cheery greeting.
His second asked what time his dinner was due.
His third asked if he could set up a Twitter account.
His fourth were to politely decline an offer
To appear on *Celebrity Big Brother*.

He was taken to lunch by a BBC producer
And shocked everyone by ordering
Marinated oven-baked gazelle drummers.

Reports came in from Andover
Of a badger which spoke in Cockney rhyming slang.
But they were just trying to cash in
Because nothing much has ever happened in Andover.
I mean, not really.

There was much discussion among philosophers
On how in one act Steven the tiger
Had managed to make all the other tigers seem
Really boring.

David Attenborough said,
'Typical, you wait all your life
For the animals to speak
And then you can't shut them up.'
Scientists from Geneva undertook various tests
In order to ascertain
What the hell was going on.
According to his DNA, Steven was just a normal tiger
And to prove it, he ate one of the scientists.

A vicar from Bournemouth saw him as an omen
Of some kind of polite Armageddon
Or at least proof of omnipotence.
He said, 'I believe that you exist.'
The tiger said, 'Knock knock.'
The vicar said, 'Who's there?'
The tiger said, 'A tiger.'
The vicar said, 'A tiger who?'
The tiger said, 'So I have just disproved all
Of your theories.'
And then he ate him.

The only thing that comes close to this
Is an elephant in 1932
But it mumbled in the most part
And sounded very nasal
And never said anything terribly interesting
And it borrowed a fiver from my uncle
And didn't pay it back.
It wasn't such an eloquent elephant.
I went to the doctor. I said, 'Doctor,
People keep thinking I'm former French
Foreign minister Dominique de Villepin.'
And the doctor said,
'It might help if you take off the name badge.'

Twitter went mad!
Hashtag conversational tiger
Hashtag rather pleasant big cat
Hashtag orange stripy anecdotage
Growly teeth snarly vicious vicious verbosity
Hashtag slightly camp when you think about it
Posh tiger dot com
Probably against the laws of nature dot com
Press the red button now to see it holding court
With Richard Dawkins and Stephen Hawking and Clare Balding
Endorsing Heinz warthog soup
And prime rib of zebra.

Tiger tiger burning bright
In neon on a Saturday night with a cheesy grin
And a thumbs-up
Advertising J Arthur Bower's Synchro Boost Houseplant
Compost
And he's standing in for Ken Bruce all next week on Radio 2.

He went on *Panorama*.
He went on *QI*.
He told a very funny joke about a
Council planning enforcer, you really had to be there.
He mauled Joe Pasquale and was roundly applauded.
He went on *Question Time* and made some comments
Which won him favourable remarks from the *Daily Mail*
Then he spontaneously combusted.
The end.

WHY I AM NOT A PAINTER/DECORATOR

(for Frank O'Hara)

I am not a painter/decorator, I am a poet.
Why? I think I'd rather be a painter/decorator,
But I am not. Well,

For instance, Jim Shufflebottom
Is doing some skirting boards. I drop in.
'Help yourself to a cuppa,' he says.
I drink; we drink. I look up.
'You've dribbled some paint on the lino.'
'Yes, I'll clear it up in a minute.'
'Oh.' I go, and the days go by,
And I drop in again. He's still doing the
Skirting boards, and I go, and the days go
By. I drop in. The skirting boards are
Finished. 'Where's the bit where you dribbled
On the lino?' 'I used some sanding paper
And white spirit and I removed it,' Jim says.

But me? One day I am thinking of an
Animal. A dromedary. I write a
Performance poem about dromedaries. Pretty
Soon it's a three-minute slam poem, and then a
Five-minute piece. There should be so
much more to it, not of dromedaries:
Of words, of how terrible dromedaries are,
And badgers. Days go by. I learn it by heart.
I am a real performance poet. My poem is finished
And I haven't mentioned dromedaries yet.
It's twelve minutes. I call it 'Poem'.
And one day I see Jim and he's doing some
Plastering, and he's got some on the lino.

POEM

Hot hot surfer dude
Dancing on the wave.
Hot hot surfer dude
You live a life I'd crave.
Hot hot surfer dude
You are so very brave.
Hot hot surfer dude
Watch out for that walrus!
Hot hot surfer dude
I'd invite you back to my
Beachfront surf shack
But you'd probably drip
All over the linoleum.

POEM

I put down my glass of wine.
The border of Devon and Somerset
Went right through it.
Shimmery non-existent man-made
Political boundary
Dissecting my Merlot,
Which knows neither the gruff sideburned
Yokelism of Somerset
Nor the soft Devonian burr
Of the barn-weary milkmaid.
I nudged my friend Jeff
To tell him this
And he spilled his lager
Right on the same county line.
And then two workmen
From competing councils arrived
To clean it up,
Their fingers, momentarily,
Fumbling together
Like mating octopuses.

POEM

You may have been an octopus
But you were always the girl for me.
I think it was on our third date
That I realised you were an octopus
When you showed me your tentacles.

I always was a sucker.

You'd put your arms around me
As we were watching TV
And still you'd be able to make a cup of tea
And do the Sudoku.
You said that men could never multi-task.
I said, 'True, guilty as charged,
We just concentrate real hard.'
You said, 'Men can't squeeze into milk bottles either.'
I said, 'That's just weird.'

I offered you marshmallows,
You offered me some plankton.
I offered you some Chardonnay,
You offered me some plankton.
I offered you some calamari,
You said, 'That's my aunt!'
It was at this moment I began
To have my suspicions
That you were an octopus
And not a receptionist from Ipswich.

You are so squishy.
Let's make sushi!
Nothing finer than watching
The *EastEnders* omnibus
With an octopus.

Nuzzling now, tentacles moving,
Writhing, gooey mass,
And those big round dots
All over my bare flesh

Where your suckers have been.
Marvellous mollusc,
Do it again,
Marvellous mollusc,
Do it again,
Sensuous mollusc,
Camouflaging yourself against the
Tartan backdrop of my bedroom curtains.
Where are you?
Where are you?
I can see you!
Okay, let's make out in the bath.

Slimy octopus ooze on ooze,
Limbs and arms and half an hour
Of just one
Enormous
Fumble.
Rhythmic writhing of bare skin
On brine,
And a sly squirt of ink
In this, the great embrace,
A cuddle times four,
Spasmodic osculating octopus
Oscillating in the sheer octopussy
Lip smack beak kiss
Squid-like romance being
Slithered on in eight
Separate
Places
Oh oh oh oh oh oh oh oh!
If this is straight sex
Then I think I like it!

Last Thursday you gave birth
To twenty thousand eggs.
They're in the fridge.

POEM

I put all of my emotions
Into containers.
My hopes and my dreams and my fears
In containers.
And I placed them before a
Grizzly bear
Who snuffled his big wet nose
On the box which interested him
The most.
I opened it, eagerly excited,
Only to find it was the one
I had put my lunch in.

POEM

I have probed the depths of literature
But my friend Mark only remembers
The one poem I wrote.

The one called 'Plop'.

And it goes something like this:
Plop.
Pah-lop.
Plop.

At nights, I reach right in and thrust my hand
Deep into the fiery furnace of metaphor,
And I grab the human condition,
And I throttle it,
And I squeeze the truth out of it,
And I tear the words from the sky,
And I wrestle with sentences like a demon.
I am the King of Ink, Monarch of the Pen,
My nib moving faster and faster as my fingers
Grip the shaft of the biro,
Spilling on to the page beauteous visions,
Truth, honesty, existential angst,
And what it means to be alive.

And yet, Mark's favourite poem of mine is
Plop.
Pah-lop.
Plop.

POEM

Lola's got a monkey.
It's a macaque.
She dresses it up in costumes
And little hats.

The other day it got out
While dressed as a traffic warden.
I saw it running up the back lane
With its little notebook and satchel
And Lola in hot pursuit shouting,
'Come back, Kenneth, come back.'
(It's called Kenneth.)

'Good luck, Lola,' I said,
'In getting your macaque
Back.'

Ten minutes later I saw her again
With a real traffic warden in her arms.
'Lola,' I said, 'Lola,
That's...'
'I know,' she replied,
'But he probably won't poo everywhere
Like Kenneth does.'

DICTIONARY FOR DUCKS

A–P
No entries.

Q
Quack
Everything.
Everything that can ever be said.
Existence.
Greeting.
Exclamation.
'Hey there.'
Quack. Answer.
Quack.
Pontification and joke.
Warning.
'How's it going?
There's some nice bread over here.
Bloody hell, isn't it boring
Being a duck?'
As in
'Quack quack quack quack.'

R–Z
No entries.

POEM

My parents are so dull.
If they were a city,
They'd be Hull.
If they were a part of a ship,
They'd be the hull.
If they were a children's entertainer,
They'd be Rod Hull.
If they were in Eurovision,
They'd score null.

POEM

I know rice.
I know chickpeas.
I know couscous.
But I haven't got
Much of a sense
Of humus.

POEM

I'm a randy lighthouse keeper.
I stop the ships
From going on the rocks.
I haven't had it off in months.
My only friends
Are the moths.

I live on a promontory.
I haven't got an internet connection.
It's the job I've wanted to do
Since the day I was born.
I have a room in which
I keep my porn.
You can hear me at nights
Blowing on my foghorn.

I like big jugs
But the only jugs I see
Are those in the sea
Washed up on the rocks
From a ship that sank
While carrying a cargo of jugs.
I should have sent it a warning
But I was too busy masturbating.

POEM

I'm in love with a monk.
His name is Brother Aloysius.
I think he's delicious.

Whenever I get in a funk,
I think of my monk
Sifting through all of life's junk
With his services and devotions
Which he's not allowed to bunk,
What with being a monk.

He's such a hunk.

He's the hottest thing in the history
Of the monastery.
I mean, in all honesty
I'd rather be
With he
Than Stoke City FC's
Ryan Shawcross,
Who's also a hunk.

Last Thursday I
Crammed myself into a crate
And mailed it to the monastery
But they delivered it in error
To a canoe warehouse.

POEM

Every time I've had sex I've thought,
My God, this is actually quite boring.
It needs livening up a bit.
It needs that extra kick.
What I need is a really good fetish
And I don't mean just
Looking forward to it being over
And having a nice cup of tea.

My mind drifts
And as we really get into it,
I start to think about things
Such as,
What's the point of lampshades?
Who first decided to make a cake
From a carrot?
And what's the big deal with
Trainer socks?
Socks to make it look like
You're not wearing socks.
I don't get it.

Liam liked it when I licked
His earlobes.
'Hubba hubba,' he'd say,
'I like it when you lick my earlobes.'
Brad liked Sellotape.
On his nipples.
Josh liked doing it
While listening to a CD of ice cream van
Music.
I'm not going to tell you what he did
To my Mr Whippy.

James liked zookeeper uniforms.
'It's the hat,' he'd say.
'The hat. Oh my God.
The hat.

Now come over here, big fella,
And help me round up the yak.'

Sex is so boring.
Sex is so monotonous.
Except for that time
I had to impersonate a hippopotamus
For James in his
Zookeeper uniform.

There's nothing more embarrassing
Than when your mind starts to wander
And the person you're doing it with
Says, 'Hello,
I'm still here.'

It's even worse
When they send a text message.

Zane would wear
Star Trek Mr Spock ears
And pronounce the whole thing
Illogical.
And just like his ears,
He had a point.

Ben liked wallpaper.
Not putting it up, but tearing it down.
With his teeth.
OMGA, we got thrown out of
So many branches of Travelodge.

Matt liked making soup
And he'd stir it and add seasoning,
Stir it and lower the heat,
Stir it and add ingredients,
Stir it and lower the heat
While I read the paper.

Lee liked football gear.
'It's my way of pretending,' he said,
'I'm someone I'm not,
Even though I am,
And in fact I am more so
Than the person I'm pretending to be,
Elevated above the masculinity
Denied by my peers and nullified
By the fact that I'm the kind of man
Who likes the kind of man
Who doesn't like the kind of man
That I kind of am.'

Two months later
He was thrown out of Wembley.
The doctor says I have a
Fear of commitment.
I can't make his appointment next week.

I went to the bank and
Asked for a statement.
The cashier said,
'My name is Jeff.'

My wardrobe wants to be in soap operas
But I've seen its acting.
It's very wooden.

But as for me, it bores me
And no matter how he adores me
I like my sex plain.
I know it's a shame
That again and again I should
Be just the same,
Just you and me and the
Promise of a cup of tea.
Brewed in a china pot
And poured from porcelain,

Flavoured with a splash of milk,
Oh, a sultry splash of milk,
The tiniest splash, from a
Bone china jug, oh that
Sexy little bone china jug,
Brewing in the pot,
Brewing in the pot,
The water dissipating and straining
Tea leaves
Pouring into thin dainty mugs.
Oh, how I look forward to that
Comforting cup of tea,
All the time wondering why
I haven't got a fetish.

Our hands fumbling in foamy bubbles
As we both do the washing-up.

POEM

Imagine my surprise
The last time I walked in the park
That someone's dog
Had the exact same name as me.

And instead of shouting,
'Here, boy! Here, boy! C'mon, boy!'
As dog-owners are wont to do,
They kept shouting,
'Robert! Robert! Robert!
Robert Garnham!
Robert Garnham!
Robert David Garnham!
Fetch the ball, Robert Garnham!
Fetch the stick, Robert Garnham!'

The whole episode was somewhat
Unsettling.
I went home and pondered on
The spontaneity of the universe
Only to get a furious email
Asking me why I hadn't fetched the ball
Or the stick earlier that day in the park,
And whether I would like
Meaty chunks for dinner.

Surely, there had to have been an error,
But when I looked up in the mirror
I was a cocker spaniel.

POEM

Slow down, Julie.
So fast, you fling the car around
Like it's a rag doll and you're
A Jack Russell,
Or perhaps it is love
That you are biting into,
Our love. You've sealed our fate
With your recklessness; you can't wait.

So, so fast,
It can't last.
As the English countryside blurs past
Into a meaningless green,
We will run out of England, soon.
Hedgerows hiding calamity
At every junction.

I bet you haven't even packed
Luncheon.

Villages with improbable names.
Finch's Bottom.
Christmas Pie.
Bathroom Tiling.
(That one might have been
An advertisement for bathroom tiling,
Come to think of it.)
Determined, you grip the wheel
And grit your teeth.
I venture some whimsy.
It falls as flat as we
Might be
If we were to hit a tree.

Slow down, Julie.
Country lanes and single-track
Carriageways and pathways,
Little more than bridleways.

Dextrously, you aim your car
As if we are rebels on the Death Star
Shooting laser cannons at
Grey sci-fi nonsense,
Imperialist forces, Darth Vader's fighter ship,
Squirrels, badgers,
Lanes passing by with inches to spare,
Like Luke Skywalker,
And you, brave Starfighter taking chance
On oblivion and the universe
In your Toyota Yaris.

A hundred and fifty-eight miles of anger driving.
We stop at an Americanised diner
Near a quarry in the middle of a
Dark featureless plain where the sky is lit
An eerie green by someone else's
Industrial units.
Your wrists ache from clenched
Gear changes.
A dank dark night with man-made weather,
A strange deserted diner on the A3-whatever.

The darkened windows reflect
Us back at us.
I raise an apologetic eyebrow
But only to myself.
You still look grumpy.
The waitress comes over,
She's a proud grey-coloured
Thoroughbred race horse,
She takes our order and
Clops off to the kitchen.
'What is it?' I ask. 'How can you still
Be so irked?'
And then it strikes me.
Hang on.
The waitress was a horse.

And so's the chef,
Expertly holding a spatula
Between his teeth,
An old English cart horse
Cooking dinner and swishing flies
With his tail.
And so's the other waitress.
They share a joke in the corner,
Whinny, and get back on with their work.

Everywhere I look, horses.
A horse at the next table.
A horse on the slot machine.
Horses perusing the menu.
Horses parking cars.
Two ponies sharing a large ice cream.
Deeply in love, she wants to
Take it to the next level.
Whoa, he's saying.
Whoa.

The place is calm, settled,
One might even say stable.
You begin to relax.
I look at you ever so briefly.
There's a flicker of a smile.

Our dinners are passable,
Though there's rather more hay
Than I'm used to.
I ask the waitress if I might
Substitute an item and have an egg instead.
She says no,
As is her wont,
For horses are notorious
Naysayers.

As we eat,

Another horse comes in,
Accompanied by a psychoanalyst.
'Why the long face?' the chef asks.
'Yes,' the psychoanalyst says,
'I'd like to know that, too.'

And then the waitress asks the chef
Why he isn't wearing his hat.
'I'd feel overdressed,' he says.
'I normally only wear jockeys.'

And then one of the waitresses
Tells the chef that she saw a zebra
In the next village.
The chef replies that it was probably
An escaped prisoner.
He calls the police.

A horse comes in.
Wearing a onesie.
A human onesie.
It makes him look like a cartoon human.
The chef is agitated, comes over
To our table, asks if
We are offended.
No.
We are not offended
By this pantomime human.

You look happier now, Julie.
The place has a surreal magic.
The horses get inquisitive and gravitate over,
We feed them carrots and apples,
And they laugh and joke
About how silly humans are
With their weathermen and their tractors
And their supermarkets and their chip shops,
And then they dance in a rhythmic clip-clop,

And we join in as the day
Bleeds into the next, dancing,
Laughing, horsing around.

Because life is written in the levity.
Our time here is miniscule, a brevity,
Into which the blessing of breathing
Is recognised only with our leaving.
We put on our coats, say our
Farewells, not understanding the world
One iota.
Heading back across the car park
To your Toyota.

And your driving is much
More sensible
As the night and the world
Seem to hug us into
Someone else's new-born day,
Looking forward to getting home
And hitting the hay.
What were you so angry about, Julie?
What were you so angry about?
Neither of us can remember any more
But we both understand ourselves
A little better.

AFTERWORD: I OWE IT ALL TO PROFESSOR ZAZZO THIIM

I've been writing poetry now for the best part of ten years. Yet my journey into the world of 'comic' verse did not come completely by accident. There is one man who came before who showed me that performance poetry was a real art form and worthy of investigation. Indeed, when people ask who my influences are, (which, come to think of it, has only ever happened once), I often reply, 'The Pet Shop Boys in a large part, but to a greater extent, Professor Zazzo Thiim.'

Who was Professor Zazzo Thiim?

Notwithstanding several attempts by many in the Californian poetry community to attribute the invention of performance poetry to their particular clique, or the claims of those within the British poetic movement to assign invention of this genre to those from various diverse backgrounds both cultural and symbolic, from Edith Sitwell to Ronnie Corbett, there remains a theory within the English departments of some major university establishments that the invention of 'performance' poetry can be traced to the moment in June 1953 when Professor Zazzo Thiim accidentally sat on a harpsichord while reciting the works of Tennyson. Indeed, it was seen as the most whimsical and amusing moment of the Basingstoke literary season, mainly on account of the audience reaction (sheer disbelief mixed with a fair amount of loathing) and the apparent embarrassment not only of Thiim himself, but also the mayor, and Arthur Miller, to whom the harpsichord belonged. There were immediate appeals for a repetition of Thiim's groundbreaking (and harpsichord-breaking) work. Indeed, he was asked to perform it on the radio (to general acclaim), and before the Ambassador to the United States (who turned out to be just a man in a hat who was passing by). Performance poetry was born.

Thiim was astounded by the fact that he had invented an entire new genre. He began writing his own verse, which he would perform either sitting on a harpsichord, astride a harpsichord, while playing a harpsichord, while lying on a harpsichord, or, finally, while lying underneath a harpsichord. This lasted for six years, until a colleague is said to have inquired of him, 'What is it with you and all these bleeding harpsichords, anyway?' He turned up at the next poetry event with a mouth organ.

Throughout this time, not only did Thiim write poems to fit in with his harpsichord-smashing regime, but he also began to dissemble and play around with the poetic form. Working in unison with the University of Staines, he looked at poems in more detail than any other literary practitioner until he acquired a reputation as a literary and poetic experimenter. Poems were shot from cannons. Poems were jumped up and down on. One poem was whispered to the Queen, who was asked to 'pass it on'. (She didn't.) One poem, entitled 'Frank (23½ Seconds of Silence)', was performed as twenty-three and a half seconds of silence. And another, 'Frank (23½ Seconds of Silence with a Brief Interlude)', was an extended version of the first but with a slight clearing of the throat in the middle. 'Frank' was a poem performed accompanied by a tambourine with the eminent professor repeating the word 'scones' over and over, finally ending with the consumption of a whole scone live on stage, while 'Frank' consisted of the professor shouting out the words 'I do not believe in Aberystwyth' while pouring yoghurt over his head. One of his most famous poems, 'Frank', received some notoriety when it was discovered that it had been the last work read by Tony Blackburn before his debut on Radio One. And of course, who can forget the stirring moment when one of his better-known poems, 'Frank', was included in the first space probe sent out by the Belgians?

There has been some question as to why the professor should have titled all of his poems 'Frank'. But as the good professor has pointed out on numerous occasions, all titles are essentially meaningless and spoil the anticipation of a poem or a work of art. Just look at 'Last of the Summer Wine'. 'Frank' seemed as good a name as any.

Do we enjoy the professor's poems today? Naturally. As the performance poetry scene goes from strength to strength, the work of Professor Zazzo Thiim has been cited by many, including myself, as their main inspiration for taking to the stage. In areas where performance poetry is popular, there has also been a marked increase in sales of harpsichords, and there can be no other reason why this is so than the enduring legacy of Professor Zazzo Thiim.

THANKS TO

There are loads of people, actually. But I should probably mention Bryce Dumont, Tim King, Chris Brooks, Jackie Juno, Daniel Haynes, Ian Beech, John Samuel, Croydon Tourist Office, James Turner, Richard Thomas, Ziggy Abd El Malak, Saskia Tomlinson, Russell Thompson, Clive Birnie

And in real life, Mark Tunkin, Damian Rao, Anne Hammet, Steven Aske.

And in family life, Mum and Dad, and Angela.

POEM

If the most obvious explanation
Is the most likely
Then why do I presume the worst?

Apricots.

Admiring the smaller moments over the large,
And always being optimistic
That all the small moments build up and become much bigger.

Thunderry showers.

I bland into the blandground,
Overlooked and quite bland
In the blanding bland bland of the bland.

Maroon.

Grabbing at several things simultaneously.
Surreptitiously.
Bland.
Obvious.
Optimistic.

Badminton
Shuttlecock.